Tangled Up
In The West

Tangled Up
In The West

A Collection of Poems about
Farming That Will Grab You Where
You Least Expect it

David Haskell

Wasteland Press
Shelbyville, KY USA
www.wastelandpress.net

Tangled Up In The West
by David Haskell

Second Printing – April 2010
Cover Design and Drawings by John Kloss
ISBN: 978-1-60047-190-2

Printed in the USA

Acknowledgments

I would like to thank my wife and son for their understanding when I had to go to the studio to work on this book. My studio being the front seat of my pickup where I smoked cigars and drank beer to get the creative process going, and to walk the tracks to recite out loud and memorize the poems.

I want to thank Myrna Bagge for believing in Piggy Smith and me, and providing the support that helped make this book happen.

And I especially want to thank my artist for recognizing my perspective, and helping me define my message. He showed me how to build a relationship with my audience by giving my poetry a time and place.

This book is dedicated in memory of Tony Mongalo. He never had a bad day in his life and he challenged us to do the same.

CONTENTS

Tangled Up in the West

Preface

The journey is more significant than the destination. And how the journey is made can bring more meaning to life. The willingness to follow the paths less taken can lead to places one never expected to go. Man's first enterprise, farming, is the closest occupation to the journey itself. Every season is different as the farmer is forced to work with an unforgiving partner that cannot be controlled. But humor is one of the "fruits of labor" that comes with working with Mother Nature. It is the balm that helps the farmer accept the adversities of his trade. These are some of the elements of farming that attract the author.

But the reality of farming is that in order to acquire enough land to farm, you have to either "marry it" or "inherit it". Unable to do either, the author cannot escape his bureaucratic job. He is tangled up in his farming dreams and the frustration that he can only exist on the periphery as a passionate observer.

A Hard Way to Make a Living

PIGGY SMITH

The tractor cabs piled along his driveway,
Mark the entrance with boneyard charm.
Inside, a group of faded red buildings,
The last remnants of the family pig farm.

But the fields around the site are empty.
The dismantled chassis have been hauled away.
And the salvaged tracks, rollers and pony motors,
Are being cured like hams for the holidays.

The dusty gravel is now covered with concrete.
The cracked plastic is gone from the counter top.
And the white linoleum floor in the show room,
Makes the office look more like a butcher shop.

But don't let the blond and the palm tree fool you.
This man makes his living selling pre-owned rust.
Offering choice cuts of used farm machinery,
From origins you hope you can trust.

The honey voice of his niece welcomes you.
She reads the "specials" and takes your parts order.
Piggy Smith's is rated four stars for ambience.
And he was written up in the *Junkyard Reporter*.

It's Piggy Smith's business philosophy,
"Make'm squeal the first time they come in.
You have to train these farmers just like weaners.
To eat whatever feed is left in the bin."

The counter man seems to be in a big hurry.
He drops my part on the scale with a clank!
He quickly slides the weights on the scale arm.
And adds another item in the deposit for the bank.

Paying twenty dollars a pound for rusty pig iron.
It's enough to make a grown man scream.
Selling USDA cuts marked prime.
This pig farmer's son, has finally seen the green.

His dismantlers pick the carcasses clean,
And his parts men sort out the best.
They tag the parts that are genuine,
And then they scrap-out all of the rest.

But he personally settles every equipment buy.
It's the "wheeling and dealing" he likes most.
Where folks only see a tired old sow,
Piggy Smith sees hidden cuts of lean pork roast.

So don't sell the family *Cat* to this butcher.
Try and find another buyer, somewhere.
Because he'll convince you, he's doin' you a favor.
But that favor is just a well-hidden snare.

"Used *Cat* parts aren't selling like they used to.
The collectors have come and skimmed off the cream.
Left me with piles of yellow scrap metal.
And now making any money is just a daydream."

"But I would like to help you with the broken D2.
Even though I have several rusting away.
Haul it over here and let me take a look.
Maybe it might be worth something, someday."

So how did Piggy Smith make a small fortune,
Selling parts from broken down machines?
He knew which parts are worth more than the whole.
And sold them like fine cuisine.

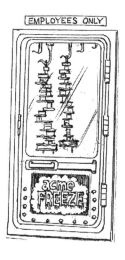

THE WEEDS ARE STREETWISE

Born in the Valley's sugar beet slums,
Enduring the Eptam[1] water-runs.
Dodging hand-hoes and bed knives.
The weeds grow up streetwise.

Their parents survived the herbicide skid rows,
They learned to make it, anyway the wind blows.
And their children knew when their leaves uncurled.
They would be unwelcome guests in a monoculture world.

With lillistons[2] chasing them down the beds,
Survival is the only thought that's left in their heads.
So they learned to hideaway in the plant row,
And hang out in the ditches where the tail water goes.

Now those shady Solanaceaes, *hairy* and *black*,
Lead an army of seedlings on bivouac.
Soon army fatigue green covers every bed top.
Another farmer just lost his tomato crop.

The weeds know all the survival rules.
They graduated from the UC herbicide schools.
Decorated veterans of many weed wars,
They terrorize their cultivated ancestors.

---

1 The brand name of a herbicide formulated by Stauffer Chemical.
2 Cultivation equipment that features a rotary hoe.

THE WEED EXPO

Mother Nature went shopping at the Weed Expo.
She had some niches she was trying to fill.
And with all these genetically modified crops.
Starting new infestations was a real test of skill.

A popular method of organic weed control,
Had the poor lady up against the wall.
Because the native tarweeds she tried to grow,
Are now covered with a new shopping mall.

She checked out the Composites Pavilion.
Their booth is usually the largest at every show.
She was a firm believer in airborne dispersion,
With an unhardened seed that is ready to grow.

The 2006 groundsel looked good this year.
She needed a winter annual to infest dormant hay.
With its toxic alkaloids and wind-blown seed,
It was guaranteed to cause any good farmer dismay.

She walked past the Shady Solanaceae's booth.
How can you trust their trade show claims?
Harry and Black were peddling the same old genetics,
Riding on the shirt-tails of the family name.

She was impressed with the improved puncture vine.
The hardened spine could now puncture a four-ply tire.
And they added a year's dormancy to the seed.
She could start infestations that were bound to inspire.

The "What's New" booth was really popular this year.
Everybody was claiming resistance to glyphosate salt.
And with a few shaky trials to back their claims.
It was a new "snake oil"; who could find them at fault.

She's been trying to promote native weeds,
Because the foreign invasives were getting such bad press.
Mother Nature is concerned with her public image.
She didn't want any tabloid headlines causing her distress.

But *Conyza* was the talk of the Weed Expo.
Better known by the growers as "marestail".
Was it true resistance or just good niche work?
This annual is taking the Valley on a grand scale.

So the farmers and the ranchers have to understand.
A lady can't make a fashion statement with bare ground.
Mother Nature dresses to make a lasting impression,
And will use any designer that leaves the crowd spellbound.

WATSONVILLE

At Boss Farms, the amigos give Ruben a beer.
To tell them the story, they always love to hear.
How he caught a "Chevy" with the big John Deere.
"Aye, I was discing the home ranch on 129,
When I saw this cabron[1], coming in his low ride.
So I made my next turn a little wide,
And buried that disc, deep in his side.
He fought hard, spun us both around.
He must have weighed at least three thousand pounds."

Bobby is bragging again down at the Trucker's Café,
About his last fishing trip to that Monterey Bay.
"Well, I saw that bobbing orange antenna ball.
So I switched on, the diesel engine stall.
I set the hook with a hard right swerve,
And my trailer drove the car up over the curb,
And the sound of folding metal was all I heard.
Now I was a little worried, to tell you the truth.
Till that driver popped up, out of the sun-roof."

Down on the Junction, the trainmen have thought,
That Casey's fifty-footer was the largest ever caught.
They still talk about the trophy that he got.
He hooked that tired trucker one morning at five,
When the gates were stuck on Riverside Drive.
Gaffed him with the coupler, behind the driving wheel.
Gutted him on the spot, peeling back the steel.
And the berries and cherries spilled out of that van,
Like fruit cocktail from a forty-foot can.

So if you don't want to become just a piece of fish bait,
Detour around Watsonville, before its too late.

---

1 Cabron is a Spanish term for a castrated goat and is often said as an insult
to another male person.

BEARINGS, BELTS AND CHAINS

"Bearings, belts, and chains, there's really nothing to it.
And without power from a "PTO," she'll just sit."
Then he lifted the hood to check the "straw walkers" inside,
And the movement of the racks that help the straw slide.
"The wood is still good and she looks complete.
But this combine is nothing, but a working antique."
And the mechanic left me at the agronomy lot.
Where she sat parked, marked, "out of stock."

Her design was simple, but better than before.
To feed a nation that was fighting a war.
To harvest the crops and save the seed.
To build a new world the US would lead.
And her partner in this noble endeavor,
Was the farm advisor, to pull all the levers.
To translate the University's "R and D",
Into plots and trials the farmer could see.

But in the nineties, deficits rang in the U.C. halls.
So the regents let the internet, make those farm calls.
They retired many farm advisors, marked them "out of stock."
And now they sit parked at the agronomy lot.

Now today's Ag economy is a global spinning wheel.
And grocery stores sell food brought in these world trade deals.
But third world farmers are still threatened by insects and
disease.

And their crops can fail from just a shift in the monsoon breeze.
These growers are still farming with bearings, belts, and chains.
They need a simple technology to help grow their staple grains.
But where is the farm advisor to help them pull the levers.
And their knowledge of plants that may be now lost forever.

THROW YOUR SHEARS AWAY

The farmer hired me to prune his orchard,
His back couldn't stretch from the ladders anymore.
He told me pruning is needed in everyone's life,
To get rid of problems that you can't ignore.

"You will need shears made with tempered steel,
To make the cuts needed to shape a new life.
And a tall ladder made with seasoned wood,
That can bear all the stretching and strife."

"Cut out those shiny green suckers,
They'll only rub the other limbs wrong.
Like all parasitic relationships.
They only take and they don't belong."

"And cut out the deadwood and the blight,
To keep the trees free from beetles and disease.
Cut out the anger that's lingering in your life.
It can damage tender buds just like a hard freeze."

"Now the rains have started and the ground is soft.
So set your ladder with a strong hand.
And push the legs through the deceptive mud,
To reach the "plow pan" to make the best stand."

"When you climb up to the second step,
Give the ladder a shake with all your weight.
It's good to test the firmness of your set,
When a fall would not be a bad mistake."

"Cut the new growth back to one leader,
To keep the limbs focused and strong.
And thin out the branches and fruit wood,
To awaken new buds when the spring comes along."

"When you finally see the tops of other trees,
It's time to stop and enjoy the view.
The climb up this ladder is a long one,
And each year it will get harder to do."

"Sometimes the ladder can start to slip-out,
When you are standing ten feet off the ground.
And your heart rushes up into your throat,
You've only got a second to look around."

"Remember this if it happens to you,
Throw your shears away if you're going down.
Throw away your ego and your pride.
They will only cut you when you hit the ground."

"Reach out for a limb that could save you,
That extended arm can now bear the weight.
And lower yourself safely down to the ground.
It's time to pass the shears before it's too late."

AMERCO'S SHOVEL

I meet Amerco at the San Jose airport.
We were smoking squirrels on public land.
All day we worked next to the bean fields.
A young buck and this old ranch hand.

Amerco was an irrigator.
And the shovel was the tool of his trade.
Milled by the earth's resistance,
Into a two-lobed metal blade.

The shovel was his constant companion,
They held each other on the long work days.
And together they watched the mystery of gravity,
Lead the water on its search for the Bay.

The unsure water moved with baby steps,
Stepping around clods that stood in its way.
And his shovel guided it like a mother's hand,
To keep it in the furrow when it tried to stray.

But the ranch foreman gave me his shovel.
He was a rude and disrespectful man.
And Amerco struggled with a new one,
That was rough and heavy in his hands.

His worried eyes watched my boots,
Jam his companion into the ground.
But a life spent following orders,
He protested without making a sound.

The handle felt like tightly braided hair,
And was almost weightless in my hands.
It sliced the earth like chocolate cake,
Reacting to even my slightest demands.

All day he pouted for his shovel.
His face bore that same deep frown.
He was jealous it would respond to my hands,
Like a whore from the east side of town.

When I lit the final smoke bomb,
And shoved it down the last squirrel hole.
I relinquished the precious shovel,
And returned that vacant part of his soul.

Fate had given him this shovel to carry,
And with it, he found a trade that he could do.
Using one of the first Stone Age tools,
And the farming skills that he knew.

THE SANCHEZ BROTHERS

The younger brother had come for his pay check.
Saturday was usually payday at the Sanchez Ranch.
That eighty acres of leased gravel and weeds,
It was this farming family's last chance.

The ranch was a hillside homestead,
With a slope that could tire a goat.
And old well was slow on the recharge,
It could barely keep the rain birds afloat.

The older brother found an FHA loan,
To grow bell peppers for the fresh market.
But without the support of a grower's co-op.
It was a decision he would come to regret.

He had to sort and pack his daily pick,
Without cooling or chlorination.
And load the truck trailer with the hope,
It would survive a one-day destination.

But last week's pick had turned to mush,
Four hundred cartons of green-stained glue.
And the LA market just dumped the load.
There was nothing else that they could do.

To his younger brother, it was just an excuse.
Another week without any pay.
Another breach of their kitchen contract.
Another wasted season, why does he stay?

His anger flashed and he jumped his brother.
A re-match of many childhood fights.
Now fueled with an adult's anger,
He was goin to "kick his ass" alright.

Their bodies crashed into the side of my pickup.
It rocked from their frustration and rage.
And their father and I sat trapped inside,
By the despair that hung over us like a cage.

Still equally matched, they finally quit.
The younger one shouting threats as he slammed his truck's door.
And he buried us in a rooster tail of dust,
He wasn't gonna be a part of this family, anymore.

CUT THEM ALL DOWN

Let the bankers, the wood cutters come,
And fight over the crumbs.
Taxes are the only thing these trees can grow.

Because I tired of pruning from dangerous heights,
And cutting branches with fire blight,
To save the trees from this bacterial ooze.

Knowing a fatal accident could wait,
Behind every tired mistake,
When you are working in the orchard alone.

And my body carries the residue,
From every pesticide brew,
I sprayed to keep the codling moths away.

I can't sign a canner's contract,
When I know the fact,
They still haven't paid me from last year.

And my son doesn't care,
Anything about growing pears.
He likes living in the cyber world.

So let the weeds come and grow,
And I won't have to mow,
With equipment I borrowed last year.

Let's put these tired trees,
Out of their misery.
Make room for the pavement to grow.

Because I don't want to see,
A single tree.
I've put this farming life behind me.

THE LAKAY[1]

Maximo was a simple man.
He made his living working with the land.
But he had lived a full life.
You could see it in his hands.

He left his island country with nothing.
The steam freighters came and carried them away.
And dropped the survivors in Hawaii,
To cut sugar cane for a dollar a day.

When he finally joined his brother in the Golden State,
The Depression was grinding men's souls.
They followed the pickers and "help wanted" signs,
And lined up behind the Okies from the Dust Bowl.

The brothers finally settled in San Jose,
Leasing ground to start their own farm.
Then the Japanese bombed Pearl Harbor.
And war hysteria sounded a racial alarm.

When their neighbors were shipped off to "camp",
The brothers saved their farm from the looters in town.
And they made enough money during the war years,
To buy their own piece of fertile valley ground.

Maximo was a quiet man.
But when he spoke, he had something to say.
"Too much water, make the plants lazy.
They will just throw their blossoms away".

---

1 Lakay is an Ilocano word for "old man" usually said in respect. Ilocano is
a Philippine dialect spoken in northern Luzon.

He was not an educated man,
But he understood nature's ways.
The natural cycles of life and death,
And the seasons that can't be changed.

Water was his silent partner.
Together they brought the seeds to life.
And he raised strawberries and vegetables,
Along with five children and a wife.

Now it's time for him to join the water,
To rest in the same earthen bed.
Let us lay him down in this furrow,
To find the peace that is reserved for the dead.

Tales from the Bureaucracy

MY FIRST VOYAGE ON
THE GOLDEN BEAR

It was a foggy morning at the harbor,
When I saw the "Help Wanted" sign.
"Navigator Trainee Wanted,"
It was an offer I couldn't decline.

So up the gang plank I trotted,
Swallowing all of my "land lovers" pride.
Stashed my gear behind the galley.
The Golden Bear sailed on the morning tide.

The boatswain introduced me to the curious crew.
"He's another "free enterprise" refugee.
He doesn't have any sea experience.
But he says he has a bachelor's degree."

Now laden with a New Year's cargo,
Of regulations and red tape.
We entered the hazardous seas,
Just off the Big Sur Cape.

I searched for the safest channel,
And we put out storm lines.
But a storm of environmental protest,
Failed to materialize.

But Tuesday morning,
Brought a sailor's warning.
There was red in the morning sky.

The east wind freshened,
Into a thunderous squall,
When EPA gave us,
An unexpected call.

We have lost our tolerance,
We have lost our Special Local Need[1].
Halt all commodity treatments,
The EPA telegram decreed.

I can't find a compass point for steering,
I don't know where the ship is bound.
"Captain, we have lost our legal ballast.
We could capsize or run aground."

But the captain was a veteran,
He had sailed the Seven Seas.
And he gave me a fatherly grin,
As he said these words to me.

"Son, the regulatory world is round,
Not flat.
So relax,
And remember that.
And you always land,
Just like a cat."

---

1 A Special Local Need is a form of pesticide registration.

A "FRIENDLY" GAME OF REGISTRATION

My co-workers have always taunted me.
They said I didn't know how to play.
"Seven Card Stud" registration poker,
Until that game before Labor Day.

Dealt a memo from Emergency Projects,
I knew it would be a hard hand to play.
Issue an SLN^1 few stakeholders wanted.
I have to catch the wild card to stay.

My final card up was the joker,
A laughing red skull and crossbones.
A category one liquid poison.
I heard nothing but collective groans.

The best hand that was showing,
Was three organophosphates.
The joker gave a possible,
Ethylene dibromide straight.

Everyone checked on the final bet.
All of my co-signers bailed out.
Who would bluff a known carcinogen,
They began to curse and shout.

They said, "I was over tolerance,
Too many parts per million.
The walking ghost of a registration,
That would come back to haunt them."

So I cleared the chips from the table,
And they called this "friendly" game.
They were too embarrassed to keep playing,
Because I had beaten them at their own game.

---

1 A SLN is a Special Local Need pesticide registration.

THE GADFLY

The gadfly buzzes around the animal's face,
With an irritating sound, hoping to be heard.
But the beast sits, completely content.
To chew its cud with the rest of the herd.

The townspeople pull on the animal's tether.
There's work to be done in the fields.
But the beast is used to the constant tugging,
And resists every attempt to make it yield.

It is ruminating on its mission statement.
It's chewing on visions for its strategic plan.
How can it keep its stakeholder promises?
And still get the governor to understand.

Its hide is marked with the bites from other flies,
That made the animal turn his head and look around.
But these bites were made to feed on the animal's blood.
And it just keep resting on the same piece of ground.

The gadfly lands on the registrant's data volumes.
Its smells decay buried under the skin.
And it circles and rubs his wings together,
To warn of the "agenda science" that lies within.

His mandibles can bite through the layers of rhetoric.
His compound eyes can see beyond the animal's view.
He asks the questions that no one wants to answer.
Why not treat everyone fairly like they're expected to do?

His legs tickle the soft skin on her undersides,
He knows where the vulnerable spots are.
But he wouldn't disclose this information.
He knows retaliation will not get him very far.

This fly's bite can make the animal stand.
Maybe, see a better view from its upright position.
Observe a world that lies beyond.
And the townspeople that deserve more recognition.

This could become a symbiotic relationship,
If the advice is not viewed as a reprimand.
Only to support the theory of responsible regulation,
That science and politics can walk hand-in-hand.

The gadfly wants to become a team player.
He wants to gain the animal's respect.
But all flies are associated with filth.
And the fly's motives are always suspect.

The gadfly is at risk from the swishing tail,
That can sweep away promotions and travel per diems.
And memberships on policy committees.
The fly could starve on the leftover crumbs.

The gadflies will come and these flies will go.
They will continue to rise out of the manure.
Most will bite just to feed on the animal's blood.
But this fly could help the animal to endure.

MARY THE MAGICIAN

She can translate any hieroglyphic,
Into something really terrific.
And she can track down,
The missing pronoun.
She always types "I" before "E,"
Except after "C."
She's Mary the Magician.

Her eyes find their way,
Through the whiteout,
The crossed out,
Filling in the left-out.
And her Houdini hands always escape,
From the tangled correction tape.
She's Mary the Magician.

She can add another line,
Or take us back in time,
So the Department meets the deadline.
Abra cadabra her fingers "cc,"
Schatzow[1] and Reagan,
And even Kosygin.
She's Mary the Magician.

---

1 Schatzow was the head of U.S. EPA during the eighties.

ARUN THE MAGNIFICANT

Arun the Magnificent has performed for 36 years.
His high wire walking can make your heart stop.
He has dazzled audiences with his daredevil deeds.
His act is the best under the Cal/EPA big top.

The cable is strung between two legislative poles.
Pesticides must be beneficial for their intended use.
And walking the efficacy policy is a balancing act,
Between scientific judgment and bureaucratic abuse.

The balancing pole is the secret to the high wire act.
It's the data's weight and breadth that holds him on the wire.
Controls and replications and analysis of variation,
Provide the rotational inertia that walkers require.

Arun doesn't trust the surly Ringmaster.
He has had run-ins with the man before.
Once he had the elephants bump the cable poles,
When Arun was walking high above the center ring floor.

When he steps out to cross the treacherous wire,
Some folks in the audience begin to cheer.
Step over step he crosses the hundred feet of cable.
And pretends he doesn't hear the crowd if it starts to jeer.

Arun has walked the wire a thousand times,
But reaching the other side, you just never know.
He remembers what happened to the Flying Chemistry Brothers,
Someone cut the ropes in the middle of a show.

But now the walking cable is starting to stretch,
The efficacy policy is starting to fray.
And the Ringmaster thinks his act has lost its thrill.
But the audience may demand that Arun's act can stay.

JUMPING JOHN

Jumpin John was a bareback rider.
He performed his horseback stunts with pride.
He managed "DPR's"[1] assessment group,
And tried to keep us all in stride.

He held a different rein for each of us,
Some were long and some were short.
To keep our heads up and watching,
To survive in this dangerous sport.

He guided us with a soft whip.
We were all professionals in his eyes.
With different gaits and different goals,
And answers for the reasons why.

He jumped us through the assessment hoops,
With controversy licking at our sides.
Above the activists cries and the pilots jeers,
We rescued molinate[2] and methyl bromide[3].

His circus stunt was a formidable one,
To keep us prancing in the matinee ring.
Around and around in circles he rode,
Until Adm. decided on something.

But they kept us out of the center ring.
They thought our science was just horseplay.
And the crowd never rose to clap their hands,
To cheer our feats at the CAL/EPA.

---

1 DPR is the Department of Pesticide Regulation.
2 Molinate is a herbicide used in rice.
3 Methyl bromide is a soil fumigate.

BACHELOR JON

He is a man with morals and integrity,
He has never drank a "lite" beer in his life!
And he packs a quick sense of humor,
That is keener than a butcher's knife.

Jon is the Registration Branch biologist.
He gives the quail and sunfish a voice.
He puts a "face" on the toxic feeding studies,
And reminds us registering pesticides is still a choice.

Now the grateful crawdads waved their claws,
When he kicked fipronil[1] out of the rice paddy.
And the yellow-legged frogs croaked a sigh of relief,
They didn't have to testify against *CATS* big daddy.

Jon keeps us amused with his latest hunting story,
And the big one that always gets away.
But he doesn't take it all too seriously,
This man still remembers how to play.

He can spot a wild boar from fifty yards,
And a wedding ring from seventy-five.
He has respect for game that's wary.
Because he knows he could be captured alive.

He is a bachelor with peculiar habits,
Resisting all forms of masculine decay.
He is always searching for that perfect miss,
That won't make him give up his bachelor ways.

---

1 Fipronil is an insecticide.

Jon has a knack for fixing machines,
He knows how to awaken horsepower.
He's not afraid to get grease on his hands,
And he only charges two "Fosters" an hour.

He keeps his red Porsche spit-polished,
And his T-bird under the covers at night.
And all of his guns are well oiled.
He likes his toys to look show-room tight.

But the man does have an Achilles heel,
That causes even his best friends to scoff.
He tries to befriend one-armed bandits,
Thinking their friendship will eventually pay off.

So Jon's a man who really likes his beer.
The question is, how does he stay so thin?
Maybe it's those long and fibrous Iowa roots,
That let him suck it up and transpire it through his skin.

GUILLERMO

Guillermo was a cowboy,
And of this there was no doubt.
But with a new bride by his side,
He could no longer knockabout.

So he left his home in the high country,
Where a man has room to roam.
And traded it all for a vinyl chair,
With a six-lined telephone.

Now his paycheck has four figures,
With a pre-paid dental plan.
And baby-skin filled in the cuts,
The wires left in his hand.

He drinks coffee everyday till ten,
Answers "nature's call" at noon.
And when the secretaries turn their heads,
Uses the wastebasket for his private spittoon.

He had a mustache black as charcoal,
With a perfect arrowhead nose.
And legs like strips of bacon,
Stretched tight in his levi clothes.

He had the fastest draw in the hallway,
Fingers blazing in six-gun style.
And he broke the meanest secretary,
With his ten-gallon cowboy smile.

But his boots were always shiny,
As he paced the office hall.
Gone completely "barn sour,"
Trapped in his office stall.

He could no longer smell the West wind,
Nor watch those tumbleweeds blow.
Staring at the power lines,
Outside of his office window.

Now a cowboy needs fresh air to live,
And a mountain range within his reach.
So why did you take the warden's job,
Guarding grunion spawning on the beach?

LA is a poacher's town,
So we wish you the "best of luck."
But after three years of pushin pen.
Are you still "one son-of-a-buck?"

"I don't need no stinking saddle."
"I don't need no stinking horse."
"All I need is a stinking badge."
And my "357", of course."

Tangled Up in the West

MAN'S BEST FRIEND

Well, it was my first month on the job,
So how could I have known?
That 100 lbs. of black German shepherd,
Was sleeping in the roses by the road.

My pickup woke him from his favorite dog dream.
His chain had finally broke.
And he rose up for that first taste of freedom,
That wouldn't end in a sudden choke.

He lunged for the driver's side pickup door,
And his teeth burst through the dust cloud.
He flashed a set of canine incisors,
That would have made, Godzilla proud.

I jerked my arm in and hit the steering wheel.
I almost put the truck in a ditch.
Now I know why this was a walk-in account.
Who would risk making a ranch sales pitch?

A salesman building a new territory,
has to try some of those gravel roads.
And a grower at the end of one of them,
turned my day into a Tarzan episode.

When I introduced myself, he looked surprised.
"What are you doing here?
I haven't business with your company,
for at least fifteen years."

When the conversation suddenly stopped,
I realized I had parked a little far out.
And this old ranch dog started following me back.
He was looking for trouble, no doubt!

He gave me his best hardened growl,
Hoping to flush me into a run.
Now he was a sporting dog.
He just wanted to have a little fun.

When I finally decided to make my move.
He thought he could beat me to the truck.
Then his dysplasia suddenly acted up.
Finally, a bit of good luck.

How I hate these home deliveries,
But the customer is always right!
He wants to spray the apricots tomorrow.
So he wants his chemicals tonight.

His instructions were plain and simple.
"Honk the horn when you first pull in."
"I'll make sure the dog is in the house"
"The dog is my wife's and he doesn't like men."

When I arrived I gave the horn a toot.
But I didn't hear a single bark.
So I guessed that the coast must be clear,
and I ventured out into the dark.

I grabbed the deadly cargo from the back of the truck,
Four gallons of ethion[1].
This is going to be easier than I thought.
Five minutes, and I'll be gone.

I started out for the front porch light.
Then I heard a backdoor slam.
And a dog's nails clicking down the driveway.
Trouble was coming, forget the telegram.

---

1 Ethion, a liquid organophosphate insecticide.

My mind froze in confusion and fear,
But my fingers held on real tight.
If I dropped those pesticide bottles here.
I'd turn his driveway into a hazmat site.

The dog kept barking, but he didn't bite.
And he skidded to a sudden stop.
When the grower arrived for a late rescue.
Boy, I was ready to drop.

You know, I have often sat and wondered,
Why that dog didn't try to bite.
I know they are an intelligent breed.
Maybe he saw the skull and cross bones on the box that night.

The lone pesticide salesman,
He has a "tough row to hoe".
And making peace with man's best friend,
Is the hardest sale, he'll ever know.

IDLE HANDS ARE THE DEVIL'S WORKSHOP

They said the farmer missed his morning coffee,
Everyday at the café this week.
So he must be doing something.
"Why don't you try his shop down by the creek?"

How I hate making these winter farm calls.
It can be a dangerous time!
But the bloom sprays start in February.
I've got to make the chemical sale mine.

Because he claims he can build anything,
The neighbors call him Mr. Make-it.
But the truth of the matter is,
Most of his projects turn out like shit!

His wife finally gives me a solid clue.
He's over at the Dairy Ranch.
He is repairing the air-blast sprayer.
So I decide to give it a chance.

The sprayer is parked on the tarmac,
The scrod pulled like a canning jar lid.
But it's been sitting there since Thanksgiving!
So who is he trying to kid?

Dumb luck has finally found me,
His pickup is parked outside.
I pull at the rusty sliding barn door.
God only knows what waits inside!

The empty manger is now a storage room.
Already, I've made a bad mistake.
Choking on the carbon dioxide flumes.
Now, *don't panic*, for heaven's sake.

The fan belts are hung like hangman nooses.
Carefully, I brush them aside.
And I step over a yellow metal carcass,
That was once Peoria's pride.

I headed for the flickering shafts of light,
From a smudge pot's blazing fire.
And Marilyn winked at me from the wall,
Wearing nothing, but a Firestone tire!

I approached a man working a hand-held grinder.
So I whispered a silent prayer.
Then he showered me with a tail of metal sparks.
He didn't even know that I was there!

I heard the hiss of a gas cutting torch.
Ruben was dissecting the ranch carryall.
To create a pile of new metal bones,
For some idea the boss was trying to recall.

He pointed with his torch towards the milking room,
"The patron is stripping parts off the old John Deere,
To build a shaker like the one he saw,
At the farm equipment show last year."

I slipped on a pool of red hydraulic fluid,
That was left by a severed limb.
Another casualty of the creative thoughts,
Of this farming breed of Homo sapiens.

I see a man sprawled on the floor,
Buried under the Deere's transmission.
Muttering swear words, I know he's alive.
And I know he's not having any fun.

What kind of man could lie for hours,
On that cold, damp concrete?
I asked myself while making small talk,
To the boots that he wore on his feet.

After getting nothing, but one-word answers,
I realize, he's not going to budge.
If this is how the man wants spend his leisure time.
Then, who am I to judge?

He says give him a call early next month.
But I know already that's going to be too late.
I can see my competitors are circling.
So I will return again and accept my fate.

How I hate making these winter farm calls.
You never know what you might stumble onto.
Idle hands are the devil's workshop.
And they might just be the end of you.

NEW BUSINESS ISN'T ALWAYS GOOD BUSINESS

Now the pesticide salesman,
He has a "tough row to hoe."
Trying to reckon a farmer's financial worth,
When even the farmer's wife may not know.

The color of his machinery,
Could be handy clue.
If there is rust flaking off it,
His pockets might be filled with it too.

And those tires with deep rubber,
Attached to that shiny green tractor.
Might only mean his cousin's a tractor dealer,
That can't say "no" to someone whose family.

And those 80 acres of sandy loam,
He fondly calls the "home" ranch.
Well, mama moved out five years ago.
He might have lost it in a refinance.

So if that new account reaches five figures,
And the last payment is 90 days past due.
And your supervisor is beginning to wonder,
About what he is going to do with you.

Well, a man's clothes can be an indication,
Of what's really going on inside.
And the belt is what I focus on.
It is the barometer of a workin man's pride.

If the leather stays up high and tight,
And the tongue doesn't start to hang out.
Well, I have learned from experience.
The money will come, without a doubt.

But my brow begins to furrow,
If gravity gets a hold of those pants.
And the tongue starts to hangin,
Like a dog's , chasing a summer romance.

A diet of coffee and donuts,
Can only carry a man so far.
And when the days start to get shorter,
He can't outrun the calendar.

So if the moon starts rising,
Before he finally grabs a hold of his pants.
Then it's "Cash On Delivery."
With prior approval from "finance."

You better stop counting your commission,
With an account that is C.O.D.
And start planning for your future meeting,
With the sales manager of the company.

So when you are out crunching new gravel.
Sometimes it's better to hit the brake.
Because there is a risk in doing business,
With only a smile, and a hand shake.

TANGLED UP IN THE WEST

When grandpa cleared the sage a hundred years ago,
He said, "It was harder to train cows back then."
So he used four-point wire on all the fences,
To keep the neighbor's cows out and his cows in.

Then, the winds blew and the sand moved in,
Buried the fences and almost their dreams.
And what kept them going through the Depression,
Was the grass growing along a perennial stream.

The deep well was dug during the war,
When farm prices were finally good.
And when we planted the best pastures to hay,
We uncovered the wire where the fences once stood.

Now I know barbed wire helped win the West,
But now a days folks just want to get untangled from the mess.

Once I took a short-cut across a back pasture.
But I found out a little too late.
That I had taken ten feet of wire with me,
For a ride out in the interstate.

When those four points finally grabbed ahold,
Chunks started coming out of that rear tire.
With pieces flying and the tread a flappin;
My God, I must be on fire.

When the rear end spun around to greet me.
I thought, "this might be the end!"
But then the skidding stopped and the dust settled.
The sand and sage brush had saved me again!

Now I know barbed wire helped win the West!
But now a days folks just want to stay untangled from the mess.

Now my bales are usually the heaviest in the valley.
Good farming keeps the alfalfa weed free.
And my cows are gaining, but moving awfully slow.
I called the vet. "What could the problem be?"

He drove out to the ranch to take a look.
"This problem better be worth my gasoline!"
Then he told me, "You've got hardware disease.
It is the worst case I have ever seen."

"These cows got anvils floating in their eyes,
And they are looking pretty obscene.
And if you sell them for slaughter now,
They'll have to cut them up with acetylene."

Yup, the Devil's rope did help us tame the West.
But now a days folks just wonder how to get untangled from
the mess.

Now when I break open a piece of new ground,
I have nightmares the night before.
Grandpa's wire is waiting there for me,
I feel like I am marching off to war.

The disc digs it up and cuts it into pieces,
Spreading shrapnel across the new hay field.
To jam the drill and dull the swather.
I feel like I am working in a battlefield.

The shards have taken out the swather's teeth.
I'm headed back to the tractor dealer again.
"Your ranch has got the hardware disease."
The parts man says with a sarcastic grin.

Now I know barbed wire helped win the West.
But Lord help me please to get untangled from this mess.

FORTY-MILE AN HOUR ALFALFA

I still wonder what my old man was thinking.
Why he bought this ground at the bottom of a crease.
With the Sierra Nevadas to the west,
And five hundred miles of desert to the east.

The down sloping wind really owns this land.
She's a cruel landlord always asking for more.
And you know it's her coming to collect the rent,
She starts banging on the back porch screen door.

She stampeded my wheel lines late yesterday,
One mile of sprinkler pipe was on the roll.
She ran them till they jumped all of my fences.
I found them wrapped around their favorite power pole.

Now I own one thousand feet of "hippie" pipe art,
with a big "wowie" in every piece.
I guess I'll call "Scrap Iron Eddie."
He might pay extra for a nice mantle piece.

And my bales are *FOB*[1] at the neighbors again.
I can't help it if they are downwind from my ranch.
And I know they get tired of selling my hay.
I'll return the favor if I ever get the chance.

Why I keep farming,
I don't even know.
Because forty-mile an hour alfalfa,
It is the toughest hay to grow.

---

1 FOB –Freight On Board, the price of hay at the ranch.

Now some storm clouds are moving up from the south,
A little moisture would help settle the dust.
But the promise of rain was just a joke.
She swept it away with a fifty-mile an hour gust.

And she lets the dust devils play on the ranch.
Her juvenile nephews are rotten to the core.
And when they get done running in my windrows,
I've got nothing but an alfalfa eyesore.

Now the harvest ants and the horned toads,
They've got it figured, no doubt.
You just let her blow till she's tired,
And then you can just dig yourself out.

And I wish I could join those lucky horned lizards.
At least they've got somewhere to go!
Because I'm trapped up here in my pickup,
Till the landlord collects the rent that I owe.

Now I just loaded twenty tons of discounted hay,
As more *TDN*[1] disappeared in the wind.
And now my eyeballs need a good washing out.
And my brain just wishes, it would end.

How can one place have, this much wind?
Isn't there somewhere else it needs to blow?
Because this forty-mile an hour alfalfa.
It's gotta be the toughest hay to grow!

Now the roof on the hay barn left last night.
And tumbleweeds are pushin my fences down.
I think the landlord is trying to tell me something!
I think it's finally time to move into town!

1 TDN –Total Digestible Nutrients, A grading system for hay. Most of the
digestible nutrients are present in the leaves.

5UD2

Now my uncle-in-law was a generous man.
He gave us a tractor when he passed away.
A crawler they bought back in fifty-one.
The same year as my wife's first birthday.

I was excited as a boy on Christmas Day.
I had a real Tonka Toy that was mine.
A piece of equipment from their San Jose ranch,
With only seven thousand hours of working time.

I consulted the office arm-chair mechanics.
Their knowledge was questioned by few.
Some backyard mechanics and Valley farm boys,
For free advice, it was the best I could do.

There are twenty-four steps for starting a D2.
One remembered from a Cal Poly exam.
But then, he became an Ag Business major.
Because he hated getting grease on his hands.

They warned me that diesel tractor won't start,
With just the turn of an ignition key.
There was a pony motor that had to be deal with.
A foreign concept for a city boy like me.

Check the electrical and fuel system first.
That's usually what goes wrong.
And don't call for a diesel mechanic,
Or else your money will soon be gone.

If the diesel smells funny, better drain the tank,
And the filter and the injectors too.
Then re-prime the system with the pony motor.
It's a task that is not easy to do.

They said "go easy" with the starting fluid,
Even though it could be a sure start.
The cylinders could fire too early,
And that pony motor might fly apart.

So we primed the spark plugs with gasoline,
And I pulled on that flywheel rope.
To bring that tractor back to life,
on a mixture of ether, gas and hope.

We kept giving the cylinders shots of gasoline,
until a spark plug wire finally broke.
And a spark arched through that ether cloud,
I almost lost my partner in a flash of fire and smoke.

The carburetor was almost impossible to adjust.
Probably it was best to leave it alone.
Uncle had set the needle valve from experience,
And I couldn't call him on the phone.

The throttle and choke knobs were side by side,
Entwined with a spark plug wire.
And one time I shuck hands with the magneto.
I musta sounded like a hallelujah choir.

She's just a big lawn-mower motor.
How could starting her be so hard.
I've seen these old tractors running.
"What was the secret?", I asked my pard.

We ran crying to the local Cat Dealer,
With our tale of frustrated woe.
But a customer in line behind us,
Tipped us a secret, a parts man wouldn't know.

"Give her four spark plug shots of gasoline,
In each cylinder, and then give it a pull.
With a spritz of ether in the air filter,
She should start, and that's no bull."

The pony motor finally came to life,
With a sound that pounded our ears.
My God, we had finally done it.
We traded cheers and had another beer.

The pony started with the choke in or out.
But what worked best, I could never tell.
And she started better on Wednesdays.
She was one piece of mechanical hell!

The bleeder valves for the injector pump,
Were designed by an engineer with a grudge.
They say he caught his wife in bed with a mechanic,
And he turned meaner than a Mississippi judge.

We bled the filter, we bled the pumps.
Until all those bubbles disappeared.
And we cranked the diesel against compression,
To generate heat, it seemed kinda weird.

But when I opened the injector pumps,
She gulped the diesel down without a burp.
Or even a reassuring puff of smoke.
More frustration, I was ready to desert.

5UD2
I've had it with you.
I know once you were Peoria's pride.

But uncle's last wish,
Has only brought anguish.
And when he said he liked me, he lied.

OLD MAN LEVERAGE

A deal is made, the check is signed.
The new owner has paid a reasonable price.
But the tractor isn't sold till it's on the truck.
It's the last roll of the horse trader's dice.

Now the buyer seems to be a savvy fellow,
An apple grower from over on the coast.
And his truck and trailer look sturdy enough,
And the new winch, he talks about the most.

The crawler hasn't run for a few years,
And now the pony motor refuses to start.
And with those tracks and three tons of inertia,
Loading her will be half-work, and half-art.

She faces us off like a stubborn old bull,
"You're not taking me without a fight."
And with tracks to magnify her resistance,
We might have to convince her with a stick of dynamite.

We try to drag her to a better loading site,
But the spring grass sets the truck wheels a spinning.
And now we have the truck stuck in the mud.
Something tells me, "this is only the beginning."

We finally get the truck moved to a better spot,
And we use the winch to drag her uphill.
It's better to have gravity on our side.
We'll need every ally in this test of will.

With the truck wheels spinning and grass flying.
He backs the trailer up the narrow dirt lane.
And with the truck and trailer finally in position.
I got a little whiff of victory champagne.

With a jumper cable assist from my pickup,
The farm show winch has got her on the roll.
But then she stalled half-way on the trailer.
Her tracks locked up, in a rebar hole.

Now the morning has turned into the afternoon,
And my buyer looks like he's ready to break.
And my sweat is smearing the ink on his check.
This sale could be lost with one more mistake.

But there was an ally waiting to help us.
Do you recall college physics One A?
The fulcrum, the plank and applied force,
This simple machine helped me save the day.

I grabbed two poles from a broken fence,
And blocks of wood from the back of my truck.
And we pried those tracks up the loading ramp.
She flopped onto the trailer like a wounded buck.

YOU CAN'T FARM WITH AN AEROSTAR

I bought this piece of ground ten years ago,
To build some city boy dreams.
I cleared the sage and planted the seeds.
This farming, it can't be as hard as it seems.
And I got the name of a local hay farmer,
Someone I might try to befriend.
To answer all my crazy questions,
And the things I couldn't comprehend.

Now he always acts surprised,
Every time that I drive up.
Because everybody he knows,
Drives a pickup truck.
So he hides out in his shop,
Hoping I will drive away.
Until he realizes it's me,
And not some tourist from the highway.
When he finally offered me some neighborly advice,
He didn't mean me any harm.
"David, buy the pickup first!
Then start the farm."

Well, I prayed for the snow and the spring rain.
I learned that water is precious indeed.
And I learned that a farmer has to experiment,
If he is ever going to succeed.
But after four years of worry and sweat,
I am going to have to concede.
The only crop I can seem to grow,
Is a new kind of jackrabbit feed.
So I asked him, "What am I doin' wrong?
Is there something I cannot see?"
He stared at the ground, took a deep breath,
And then he told me.

"It's the car!
You can't farm with an Aerostar!"

"Now you better stay off the highways,
When those cold winds start to blow.
Because that's a California car.
It doesn't like the snow.
Or always carry your tire chains,
Flashlight and poncho.
Unless you like driving sideways,
Where ever you try to go."
And you can't park this car,
In front of any "honky-tonk" or bar,
Because everybody in town,
Will know exactly where you are."

"Now I know that sliding door opens wide,
And those seats, they do come out.
And you can fit a pair of calves inside,
From the tail to the snout.
But if you desecrate the family car,
Your wife is going to shout.
And you better not drive in the carpool,
Until all that poop dries out."

"And when you take those rear seats out,
There is plenty of room in back.
For your tools, pesticide cans,
And your handyman jack.
But, you better pray the Lord is with you,
If you ever get in a wreck.
Because that load you have been a carryin,
You will be wearing around your neck!
So you had better hire a good lawyer.
And write a brand new will.

Because if your tools don't getcha,
That 2,4-D[1] will!"

"It's the car!
You can't farm with an Aerostar!"

---

1 A herbicide the controls broad-leaf weeds.

Breinigsville, PA USA
24 March 2010
234828BV00001B/1/P

David Haskell   Poetry Performer
Tangled Up in the West

"Poems About Farming
From the Wrongside of the Furrow"

Entertainment for Conferences, Festivals
9407 Shumway Dr. Orangevale, CA 95662
(916) 989-3791   davidehaskell@sbcglobal.net